ISBN 978-1-9162995-4-2

Design of this book by Nancy Goudie and Chris Mathison. Series design by Helen Martin.

Cover and interior illustrations by Chris Mathison and Charlotte Cooke.

Published by The NGM Trust, Caedmon Complex, Bristol Road, Thornbury, Bristol, BS35 3JA. www.ngm.org.uk

Printed by TJ Books, Padstow, Cornwall

You Are
Beautiful

(Born to be significan

[Dictionary definition: Having beauty; pleasing to the senses or to the mind, possessing qualities that give great pleasure; excellent.

[(Born to be significant)
Dictionary definition: Born to be important ar noticed.

Preface

This is a book that I never thought I would write. When I finished writing a trio of books called The Beloved, Confident? and You Are Special, I said that the last book, You Are Special, finishes the trilogy and ends the series, but I was wrong! Here we are 11 years later with a book that fits the same theme as these special, unique books. The title of this book says it all

You Are Beautiful

Born to be significant.

Whether you are a man or a woman we are all unique, creative, wonderful, significant, valuable, and yes beautiful human beings. We all need to know how incredible we are. Each one of us was born with beauty and creativity in our DNA because each of us, whether male or female, was born in the image of God *(Genesis 1:27)*. We have all been put on this planet for a purpose and a reason and therefore the truth is all of us have been born to be significant.

This is the 18th book I have written and it has been the one I have had the most joy in writing. I am praying that this book will encourage and build you up, it will bring joy and revelation, and it will lift your spirit to another level. This is what it has done to me while writing this book, so I'm praying it will do this to you while you read it.

Like the other trilogy of books, it is designed to encourage and bless you. It is not a book you necessarily read in one go, but like the others is a book that can be opened at any page and no matter what page you open it at, it is designed to bless and encourage you. If one day you wake up feeling miserable, or at any point in the day you get a knock back from a comment someone has said about you, then pick up this book. Open it at any page and you will receive encouragement for your soul. You will hear the truth about who you are and no matter what anyone else thinks or says, you are born to be significant, and you are a wonderful, creative, beautiful human being.

YOU ARE BEAUTIFUL

(Born to be significant)

Hey beautiful - Yes YOU!

Did you know you are beautiful?

You were created in the image of God
and God is full of beauty so,
whether you are male or female,
you are beautiful!

You are not only beautiful,
but you are also significant
- you were born to be significant.
Don't let anyone or anything take away
your significance.

Every year at my Spiritual Health Weekend (a weekend of fun, relaxation and deep encounters with God for women) I always do a Spiritual Exercise session. Within the session, I have a fun memorising exercise. I always set it to some music we wrote many years ago, which we released into the clubs in the UK and Europe. It reached number 1 in the DJ charts. I love it because it has a regular beat which works well for memorising. This is what we memorised at my Spiritual Health Weekend in 2022..... the theme that year was You Are Beautiful.....

You are absolutely beautiful;
there is no flaw in you.

You are absolutely beautiful;
there is no flaw in you.

In you. In me.

There is no flaw in me

I'm absolutely beautiful;
there is no flaw in me!

(Taken from Song of Songs 4:7)

Memorise this and repeat it every day – maybe even several times a day and eventually you will begin to believe it to be true.

In the Bible (Matthew 13:45-46) there is a wonderful story about a merchant who came across an incredibly beautiful pearl. When he saw this superb pearl, I can just imagine him exclaiming out loud:

"I want you! You are the most perfect pearl I have ever seen. You have been created with beauty. You have been sculpted and crafted in such a way that you are perfect from every angle."

He decided to sell everything he had to buy this gorgeous, precious, wonderful pearl.

I can then imagine him going home and telling his wife, "We are going to sell everything – our home, our possessions, our furniture, in fact everything we own." His wife replied, "You are selling everything for one single pearl?" He said, "Oh but wait until you see this pearl, it is exquisite!! You will understand when you see the pearl."

When Jesus told this story, he was showing us that each of us is that beautiful pearl and that he would give everything he had to purchase one single soul. One soul is so valuable in the sight of God. Do you know that you are that pearl? You are beautiful. You are glorious. You are precious. If you had been the only person in the whole of history, then Jesus would have died for you. We have no way of fully comprehending the value that God sets on a human pearl; to him you are a pearl of outstanding beauty, and he gave everything he had for you! You have been bought with a great price (1 Corinthians 6:20a). Jesus fully paid the price so that you would become his possession. The shedding of his blood meant that he had paid the price and he now sees you as his own! He shed his blood for you – the only price that could buy you, his beautiful and perfect pearl.

Begin to see yourself as you really are – that beautiful and precious pearl that is worth so much more than you could ever imagine. I can just hear the Lord saying to each of us, "You are beautiful; you are the most precious pearl I have ever seen and although you cost me everything, I was glad to pay the price. You are important, valuable, cared for; you are significant, my special and wonderful treasure! You are mine, my prized possession; you cost me everything, but I don't regret paying the full price – not for a moment! You are so valuable. You are wonderful. You are worthy and I adore you!"

Picture yourself as that pearl and consider the vast price he paid for you!

A Pearl of Outstanding Worth and Beauty; A Significant Gem

"You are my glorious, wonderful and very beautiful pearl. A pearl is a person of great rarity and worth. I want you to know that I call you my pearl because you are a rare gem and are worth so much more than you could ever know. You are unique and highly prized like a pearl that comes from the sea. They require no special cutting or polishing to maximise their beauty and, my beautiful child, neither do you. You are complete and have been crafted and created by my hand."

A PEARL - a person or thing of great rarity and worth; highly prized as a gem. Perfectly formed in an oyster's shell.

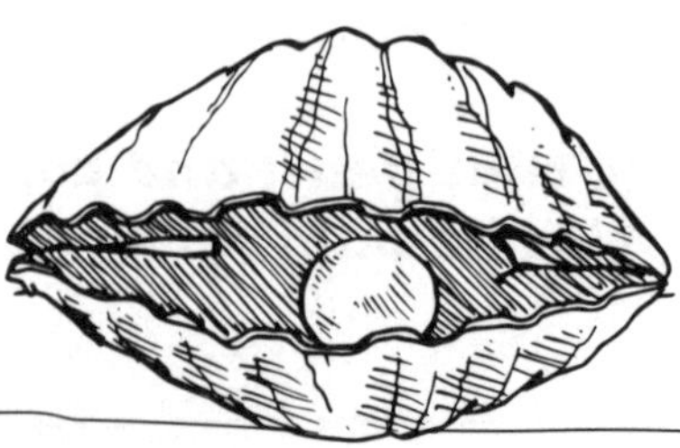

How beautiful you are my darling!
Oh, how beautiful

(Song of Songs 4:1a)

12 Beautiful things about you!

1. You are unique
2. You were created with love
3. You have supernatural strength within you
4. You were created in the image of God
5. You are beautiful
6. You are a blessing
7. You were loved before you were born
8. You have been called and chosen
9. You are never alone
10. You shine in the darkness
11. You blossom in God's light
12. You are loved in the present, loved in the past and loved in the future

What a beautiful and wonderful person you are! Never forget how significant you are!

When my husband told me I was beautiful – I could not believe him. It didn't cross my mind that anyone would think I was beautiful. I felt I had so many flaws in me. One of those flaws were my legs! I didn't like the shape of them. But unknown to me at the time, my husband fell in love with me because he loved my legs. It was my legs that originally attracted him to me. When he told me this many years later, I was stunned. A friend recently told me that I had great legs – again it stunned me to discover that they genuinely thought I had great legs. Because of these and other compliments I have received about my legs, I have begun to see the beauty in something that for years I saw as flawed. We all need new eyes to see ourselves as the beauty that we are.

I remember waking up one morning to discover Ray staring at me. His first words before I could ask him what he was doing were: "You Are Beautiful". I was shocked, I had never considered that others could see me as beautiful, but something happened that morning – something happened deep inside me – a truth was laid in my heart that I would eventually begin to believe.

Hear this today, "You are beautiful. You are stunning. You are significant. You are priceless. You are loved. You are valued. You shine. You are a blessing. You are never forgotten. You are a light on a hill that should never be hidden."

So today, let these truths begin to take seed in your heart and believe the truth about you!

Put those words on a mirror and/or on cards to keep in your purse – and when you see them repeat the truths written in each statement – whether you feel beautiful or not...and slowly the truth of these words will begin to find a lodging place in your heart.

YOU WERE MADE FOR MORE

This beautiful song was written by my daughter-in-law, Leanne Goudie. Have a read of it and discover the truth in the lyrics – you were made for more than the four walls you have put around you. God has called you to be free – to live in freedom and be significant. Live who you were meant to be – you were born to be significant!

You can be strong, you can be free
You can stand tall and be who you want to be
You can set sail into new dreams
You can be strong and be who you wanna be

You were made for more than these four walls
Just tear them down
You were made for more than these four walls
Just tear them down
You were made for you, you were made for more
You were made for more than these four walls

Take a blank page, start a new day
You don't have to stay stuck in this storybook
You can fight it, just rewrite it
You can show them all

You were made for more than these four walls
Just tear them down
You were made for more than these four walls
Just tear them down
You were made for you, you were made for more
You were made for more than these four walls

You are, you are, you are strong
You'll stand so tall and never fall
You are, you are, you are strong
You are, you are, you are strong
You'll stand so tall and never fall
You are, you are, you are strong

You were made for more than these four walls
Just tear them down
You were made for more than these four walls
Just tear them down
You were made for you, you were made for more
You were made for more than these four walls

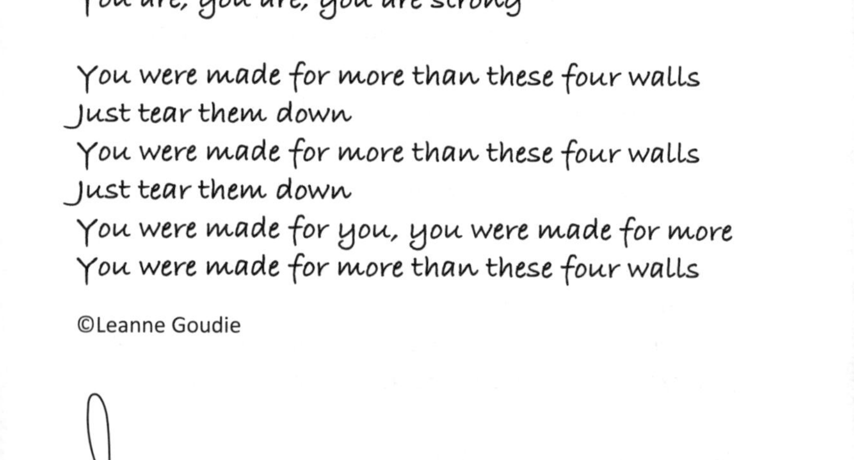

A lady attended my Spiritual Health Weekend in 2022 and, in her own words, she could not look in the mirror. She avoided doing so because she did not like what she saw. But after a weekend of affirmation and teaching about who she was, she left the weekend able to not only look in the mirror but rejoice at what she saw. God totally changed her perspective.

The truth is you are beautiful. God made each of us in his image and he is glorious, beautiful, incredible, wonderful, strong and so much more.....believe who you are; you have been made in the image of a most beautiful and awesome God.

Listen to the Lord as he expresses his love for you:

How beautiful you are. My darling! Oh how beautiful
(Song of Songs 4:1a)

How beautiful you are and how pleasing!
(Song of Songs 7:6a)

Our amazing God is our friend, our Saviour, our Lord, our partner, our husband, our lover....he pursues us with a passion so strong and a heart that does not waver. He constantly loves us with an unconditional, faithful love. Listen as these words are spoken to you today!

My lover spoke and said to me:

"Arise my darling, my beautiful one, and come with me. See! The winter is past; the rains are over and gone. Flowers appear on the earth; the season of singing has come, the cooing of doves is heard in our land. The fig tree forms its early fruit; the blossoming vines spread their fragrance. Arise, come, my darling; my beautiful one, come with me!"
(Song of Songs 2:10-13)

Let's respond right now to our glorious God, our intimate and passionate lover and walk with him as Spring takes hold of our hearts and we are drenched in his beauty and grace.

Do you want to know what beautiful is?

Look at a sunset
Look at a mountain range
Look at a sparkling sea
Look at a colourful flower
Look at a tree
Look at a pearl
Look at a diamond

Each one of these are stunning, yet none of them are as stunning as you!

You want to know what beautiful is?

Look in the mirror!

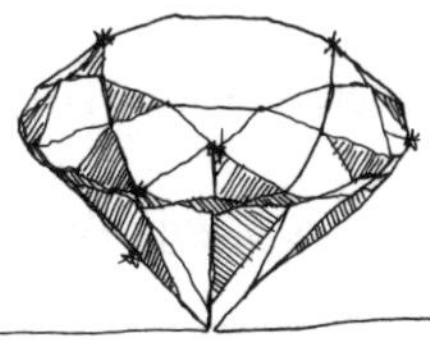

Are You Listening to the Right Voices?

There is something incredible about being in the presence of people who think you are wonderful and special....it is so freeing and so empowering. You begin to believe what they are saying about you.

When I was younger, I would not tell anyone that I wanted to be a public speaker because I thought that everyone would laugh at me if I shared my vision, so I kept it to myself for years. There were so many things that told me that I could not become an itinerate speaker.

I was brought up in a church who did not believe in women speakers (unless you were only speaking to an audience full of women!). There were no opportunities in my church for me to learn or opportunities to even observe other women preachers. I was so scared to speak in public and would only do so if it was scripted for me – like a poem or to perform a Shakespeare monologue. To think about speaking in public seemed so far out of my comfort zone. One day I had the courage to share my thoughts about my desire to become a preacher with my husband and instead of laughing at me, he surprised me by telling me that he could see that vision becoming reality. He told me, "You can certainly do it." I said, "Really?" He said "Yes" and encouraged me all the way. When others around you tell you that you can do it, that you are wonderful, that you are called and chosen, that you are beautiful, you eventually begin to believe it.

Make sure you are listening to the right voices.

I remember in my teens going to a new dentist who told me that my teeth were beautiful and that I could be in an advert for perfect teeth. He also told me that I had a great smile. I came away from that dentist appointment so encouraged. No one had told me that before. Because of those comments, I began to feel different about myself. I felt beautiful. I wanted to smile more. I wanted people to see my smile and see my teeth all because a dentist said some very kind and encouraging words and I could see that he meant what he was saying! However, when I mentioned what the dentist had said to a lady who was a friend of my mum's, she decried what the dentist had said and suddenly all that encouragement began to fade with every word she spoke. I don't know why she was so cruel to me with her words, but I never spoke for a long time about what the dentist had told me. Pick the company you keep well....because the words of others can either build you up or tear you down.

Remember this:
You are amazing and you can do ALL things because of Christ Jesus.

"My special one – you are stunningly amazing, and I will love you forever. Never forget how special, wonderful and beautiful you are!"

Special One

You're absolutely flawless
You're beautiful to me
A diamond like no other
You sparkle endlessly
Your beauty shines from head to toe
You set my heart alight
I'm with you every morning
And hold you through the night

O Special One, My Special One
Don't turn your face away
O Special One, My Special One
I love you, hear me say
I love you more than precious gold
Such beauty to behold
O Special One, My Special One is you

Don't hide amongst the shadows
Step out of loneliness
Come feel my arms around you
And feel my tenderness
Your name excites my Holy passion
And fills me with delight
Your kisses are like honey
My bride all dressed in white

O Special One, My Special One
Don't turn your face away
O Special One, My Special One
I love you, hear me say
I love you more than precious gold
Such beauty to behold
O Special One, My Special One is you

Are you believing what God thinks about you?

I heard a story recently of a school who decided to put all the names of the teachers in the school in a hat and draw one out to be called the best teacher in the school. Once they had that, they put all the names of the pupils in the school in a hat and they randomly chose 30 to be the best students in the year. They told the teacher that he was the best teacher, and they told the 30 students that they were the best students and that the 30 students were going to be taught by the best teacher for this next year. At the end of the year, the result was that this class achieved 22% higher than all the other classes. They told the results to the teacher who said – oh that's because I am the best teacher in the school. They said, "Well actually you were picked randomly out of all the other teachers in the school. It was not based on your ability." The teacher replied, "Then it was because the 30 pupils I was teaching were the best scholars in the year!" They then told him that all pupils names were put in a hat and the 30 pupils were picked randomly again, not based on their ability. He asked them, "Then why did we get such a great result?" The answer was that both the teacher and the 30 pupils believed that they would succeed and so they did!

What do you believe about yourself? Are you a world changer? Are you a history maker? Are you someone who is called and chosen? Do you know you have been picked out of a crowd? Do you know you are loved? Do you know you are beautiful? Do you believe what God believes about you?

Put declarations about yourself on a mirror or somewhere where you will see it every day – speak out the truth about who you are.

Tell yourself that you were called before the foundation of the world was put in place (Ephesians 1:4).

Tell yourself that before you were born God knew you! (Jeremiah 1:5).

Tell yourself that you are beautiful inside and out and that you are the apple of his eye! (Psalm 17:8a).

Believe what God believes about you.

The Apple of His Eye

Did you know that you are the apple of God's eye? What does it mean to be the apple of his eye?

The pupil of the eye is the most sensitive part of the body and therefore to be the apple of God's eye means that you are highly cherished and hugely protected. The Lord loves you, cherishes you, protects you, honours you, blesses you, he looks after you, he values you highly.

If you lose your sight, you lose something so valuable - did you know that you are priceless and highly valued?

For whoever touches you touches the apple of his eye

(Zechariah 2:8b)

Keep me as the apple of your eye...

(Psalm 17:8)

Did you know that God has so many wonderful thoughts about you? You are never forgotten (Isaiah 49:15), in fact if someone was to record God's thoughts about you, they would outnumber the grains of sand on our seashores in this planet. He constantly thinks about you and his thoughts are good thoughts.

You saw me before I was born. Every day of my life was recorded in your book. Every moment was laid out before a single day had passed.
How precious are your thoughts about me, O God! They cannot be numbered! I can't even count them; they outnumber the grains of sand!
And when I wake up, you are still with me!

Psalm 139:16-18 – NLT (New Living Translation)

You saw who you created me to be before I became me! Before I'd ever seen the light of day, the number of days you planned for me were already recorded in your book. Every single moment you are thinking of me! How precious and wonderful to consider that you cherish me constantly in your every thought! O God, your desires toward me are more than the grains of sand on every shore! When I awake each morning, you're still with me.

Psalm 139:16-18 - TPT (The Passion Translation)

Never forget God cherishes you in his uncountable thoughts about you……WOW!

Are you beginning to see how precious you are?
Are you beginning to see how significant you are to God?
Are you beginning to understand how amazing you are and how much God loves and values you?

Meditate on these truths and see the beauty and significance in you!

I AM WHO YOU SAY I AM

The Bible tells me:

I am precious
I am worthy
I am loved
I am called
I am chosen
I am beautiful
I am valuable
I am priceless
I am desired
I am accepted
I am cherished
I am gifted
I am amazing
I am wonderful
I am powerful
I am significant

I believe what the Bible says about me!

Lord - I am who you say I am!

BEAUTY IS IN THE EYE OF THE BEHOLDER

On many days when we drove home from our mission and arts complex, Ray would often say, "Oh this street is so beautiful. I absolutely love it!" We have a small lane which leads you from the main road to a small cul-de-sac of houses where you would find our home. Each time Ray exclaimed about how beautiful this lane was, I didn't say anything but in my mind I would think – I don't think this lane is beautiful at all. In my mind it was very ordinary, very bare, very dark and to me quite ugly. However, in the last number of months/years, I have begun to see the beauty that Ray saw in this lane. How did I not see it beforehand? I really didn't comprehend it! It was as though my eyes were closed, but one day my eyes opened and I could see the massive beauty it declared. I suddenly saw that it is a very beautiful lane filled with glorious trees and beautiful flowers and now every day I exclaim – Wow! This lane is so beautiful!

They say beauty is in the eye of the beholder and that is often so true. What one person sees as beauty another does not. It is so important to see each other through the eyes of our God. He sees how beautiful we are – inside and out! Even if you cannot see that beauty at present, speak out the truth of how God sees you and, like me with the lane leading to our home, you will begin to see the truth about the beauty in you!

YOU ARE BEAUTIFUL

When I married Ray, the two of us became one. We loved being with one another. We eventually even started working together as God called us into full time Christian work and we loved it. We never felt we saw too much of each other – we just loved being in each other's company. We loved talking to each other and would do so for hours. We loved to hold hands and walk with each other. If Ray decided to go to bed, I would very often go to bed too, because I always wanted to be near him. If we were separated for a period of time due to ministry, we would always keep in touch on the phone and our hearts would always ache, yearn and long for the time when we would be back together again. That's what happens when you love someone.

Did you know God loves you even more than Ray and I could ever have loved each other? Did you know that he loves to talk with you? Did you know that wherever you go, he goes too? He never leaves you nor does he forsake you – even when you take a wrong pathway. If you walk away from intimacy with him for whatever reason, his heart longs, yearns and aches for you. He longs for that deeper intimacy, that deeper relationship with you. He takes a hold of your hand and gently draws you back to himself. He never gives up on you; isn't that a wonderful truth? Others may abandon you, but God never does – he always seeks the best for you and pursues you no matter where you go!

WHY? Because he loves you so very much – much more than you could ever know or imagine! Be aware today of the God who delights in you, who sings over you – who rejoices in you, his bride and draws you with cords of loving-kindness.

CHOSEN

Ray chose me to be his wife and I chose him to be my husband. Why? Because we loved each other, but God chose me/you before the foundation of the world was put in place! Wow! Before I knew him, he knew me; before I loved him, he loved me. What a wonderful truth for us all to know.

For God chose us
before the foundation of the world

(Ephesians 1:4)

Before I formed you in the womb,
I knew you, before you were born I set you apart

(Jeremiah 1:5)

Being chosen makes me feel loved, accepted, special, grateful, blessed and wonderfully favoured.

My prayer is that you will feel these emotions and so many more today knowing that you are chosen – picked out of a crowd and loved even before you were born.

God chose you to be his bride. He chose you to be his intimate. He chose you to be his friend.

What's your response today to such a love as this?

You Are Very Good

God is the most amazing artist – EVER! You only need to look at the world he created to discover what an incredible artist he is. His colours, his creativity, his shapes, his sounds, his designs amaze us as we see the depth of beauty in everything he made. Not only did he fashion and create the world in which we live, but also what he did in the rest of the universe is breath-taking! Planets and galaxies were made by his design and what a design. You only need to look at the vast array of the heavens to discover what a stunning, incredible and flamboyant artist he is. Did you know that our sun is a star which is a million times larger than the earth? However, it is only one star in a 100 billion stars that make up our galaxy, which is called the Milky Way. The Lord took time and effort to create each star, for each is different in terms of size, lifetime, colour and temperature. The interesting thing is that our galaxy is only one in 100 billion galaxies in the universe! Not only that, but our sun is as small as a grain of sand when you compare it to the size of other stars! Wow!!

When the Lord finished creating the world and the universe, he looked at all he had made and said, "This is good!"

(Genesis 1:14-18)

But he didn't stop there, he went on to create the birds in the sky, the fish in the seas and animals to live on the land. He didn't just create one type of bird, fish or animal, but as an amazing artist, he created various, wonderful, colourful, extraordinary creatures. Each one is incredible. No wonder when he had finished, he again said, "This is good!"

However, then came the best bit of all! He then thought of you and me and went on to create mankind in his image! The greatest artist ever shaped, fashioned and formed human beings in his own image!! Wow! You only need to look at the human body to discover God's design is incredible and immensely beautiful. God took so much pleasure in crafting and creating mankind that when he was finished this time he said, "This is very good!"

We all need to remember that we are his stunning, amazing creation and that he looks at us individually every day and says,

"Hey Beautiful – you are very good!"

My Heart Cries Out For You!

My heart cries out: I so love you, Lord. I cannot thank you enough for your wonderful love for me. You make my heart sing with songs of joy and deliverance. You are my great and wonderful God, and I am your beautiful and glorious child. You put your arms around me and hug me to yourself. I am covered in your love and drenched in your joy. Laughter is never far from my mouth as the joy within bubbles up and overflows. Oh Lord you are amazing to me. I cannot thank you enough for all the good things you pour into me. What joy! Amazing joy! What peace! Amazing peace that passes all understanding! What life! A life that never ends and surpasses everything I have ever known and experienced. Thank you, Lord. Thank you, Papa. Thank you, Holy Spirit. Come closer still – my heart aches for you and I love to be in your presence. I adore you and love you because you first loved me! Woohoo!

How lovely is your dwelling place, O Lord Almighty! My soul yearns, even faints for the courts of the Lord; my heart and my flesh cry out for the living God.

Psalm 84:1

A Message from Papa God

"Did you know that your steps will resound throughout eternity? Did you know that when you take steps of faith – it will show thousands of others the walk of faith? Do not be limited. Do not be bound by anyone or anything because I have given you life and freedom. Instead, be confident for you are born to be significant. Significance is in your DNA! Know this: my courage and my strength are within you. My plan is your plan, and my plan is good, is full of hope, passion, purpose and prosperity and it will never fail to succeed.

Therefore, step out in faith and hear the sound of your footsteps as they echo throughout the ages! You are significant!"

Your Papa God!

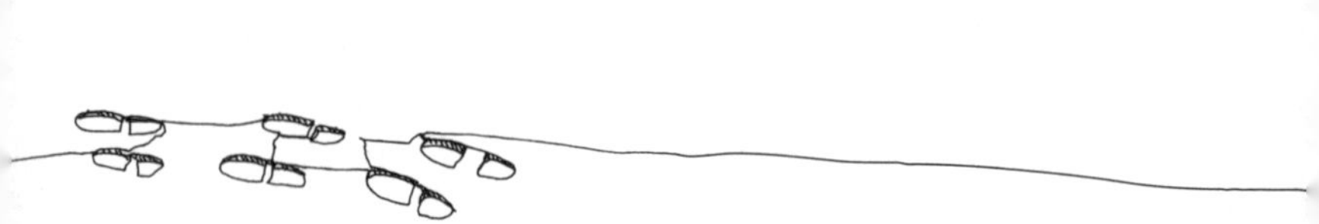

I KNOW WHO I AM

I know who I am. I am called and chosen. I am loved more than I can imagine. Wow! That is enough!

I don't lack any good thing.
He is sufficient - therefore I am sufficient.
He is significant – therefore I am significant.
I am like my Papa God – I am his offspring!

What am I lacking? NOTHING!
I have been given everything I need for life and godliness (2 Peter 1:3). He has already given me EVERYTHING – so what do I need? NOTHING! I have it all.

What can keep me from enjoying it all? A lack of trust or unbelief.

Let's not have a lack of trust or the sin of unbelief in our lives, instead let's shake off everything that holds us down and keeps us from our destiny.

Let us throw off everything that hinders and the sin that so easily entangles and let us run the race marked out for us.

(Hebrews 12:1)

How do you view God? What is your picture of God?

This is significant because the way you picture God affects your picture of you. The way you view God affects the way you view yourself.

There was a woman in the Bible who committed adultery and the male leaders of the time brought her to Jesus to see whether he would uphold the law and condemn her to death. In this story they did not bring the man who committed adultery with her, but instead only brought the woman. Did they let the man off with the crime? Was it because women in those days were thought of as second-class citizens on the same level as their cattle? A woman had no rights and were seen more as a slave rather than a valued member of society. Jesus treated women differently. He changed the way the world saw women. He honoured them, he valued them, he had women in his travelling group of disciples. He stopped and spoke to women, the first evangelist in the Bible was a woman, the first person to see Jesus after he rose from the dead was a woman. He told her to go and tell his disciples that he was alive – he gave her the honour of teaching the disciples about his resurrection and he was supported financially by rich women – all these things were unheard of in his day!

When this woman was brought before Jesus for his judgement, he didn't condemn her, instead he showed her love, forgiveness and a new way to live. He showed her that she was valuable. He invited those standing there, if they had committed no sin in their lives, to throw the first stone. The Bible says at first the older men started to walk away, then the younger ones did the same until there was no one to condemn this woman. The only person who could have condemned her was Jesus himself, as he lived a life without sin, but he chose not to do so.

Jesus showed her a new picture of God – one where love and forgiveness reigns and conquers all. That new picture of God then gave her a new picture of herself. She must have begun to see herself as loved, valued and worth more than what others told her she was worth.

What is your picture of God today? Do you see him as he is – kind, generous, loving, forgiving, full of grace, peace, joy – someone who is always looking out for you? Or do you see him as hard, condemning and unforgiving towards you? If the latter, then begin to change your picture of God by encountering the living God each day. This woman encountered the living Lord Jesus and her whole picture of God changed dramatically. She received glorious life when she was expecting a horrific death.

Your picture of God – will dramatically change your picture of you....

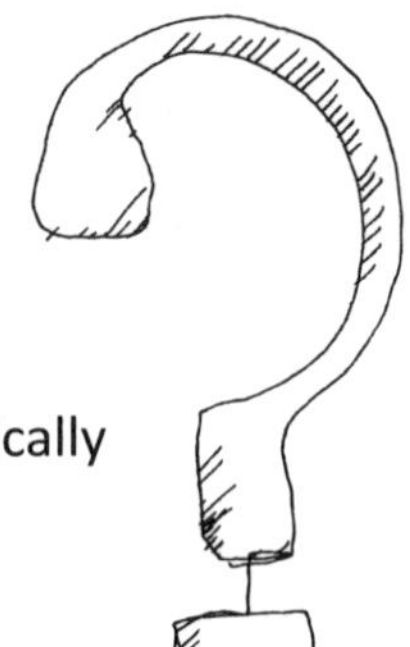

Are you dominated or haunted by mistakes you have made in life?

You ask for forgiveness, but what happens is you find that your mistake (big or small) seems to dominate your thoughts and haunt you. You re-live that incident over and over again. It could be something that happened in your past or it could be something you did yesterday. As you re-live your mistake you feel condemned, judged by your own thoughts. Even though you have asked for forgiveness from God, your own thoughts condemn you. This is when it is important to train your thoughts – reign them in with the word of God. God says that when you ask for forgiveness, he removes your sin as far as the east is from the west (Psalm 103:12). Who are you going to believe? Your own condemning thoughts or the word of God? It's at this time that we need to turn our eyes upon Jesus. Jesus is perfect theology – so if you want to know what God looks like – then look into the eyes of Jesus. He is full of love for you. He provides peace and joy for each of us (John 14:27 and John 15:11) – the kind of peace and joy that lasts forever.

Have you ever seen a baby after they have been fed from their mother's breast? They are at peace, full - because of all they have taken in. All crying has ceased and now they are showing contentment. This is a wonderful picture of us and God. The more we are fed by the love of God, the more peace, joy and contentment we will enjoy.

So today and every day, as this old hymn says: -

TURN YOUR EYES UPON JESUS
LOOK FULL IN HIS WONDERFUL FACE
AND THE THINGS OF EARTH WILL GROW STRANGELY DIM
IN THE LIGHT OF HIS GLORY AND GRACE.

Everything else fades to insignificance when we see and encounter Jesus. Encounter Jesus every day and taste of his love, joy and peace.

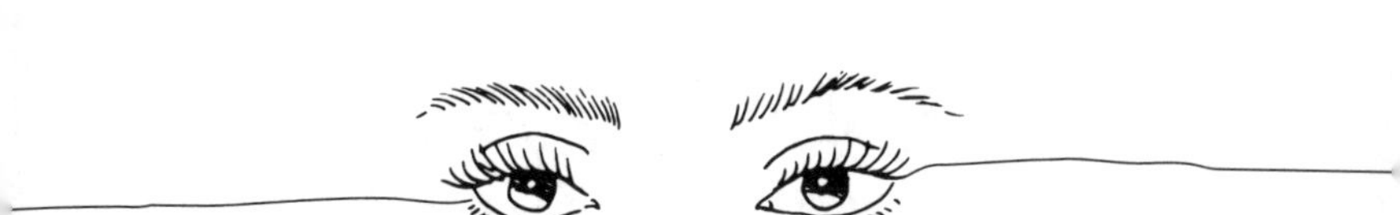

Those who look to him are radiant; their faces are never covered in shame

(Psalm 34:5).

Shame is what the enemy uses to condemn us – but shame is never from God. He never shames us – instead he invites us to look to him and become so full of his light that we are radiant – filled with his glory and grace.

So, remember to turn your eyes upon Jesus and look full in his wonderful face because as you do, you will shine with his beauty, his purity, and his grace. Woohoo!

In the Bible we can see that God called and chose people and he called them by name! Isn't it wonderful that God knows you by name? Just think about this for a moment - he knows your name! He mentions you by name! He speaks your name! I love that – we are not just a number to God, he knows us, he is intimately involved with us – he knows us by name!

In a book called Numbers in the Bible, you can see that God called the leaders by name. He knew them and knew the skills they had even before they knew their skills. He knew too the names of those who would assist the leaders. He knew those who had artistic and creative skills and told Moses that he had chosen them to make the Ark of the Covenant. He demonstrates in the Bible how intimately he knew each one.

Did you know that God knows you inside and out? He intimately knows you! He has absolutely fallen in love with you. He longs for a deeper intimacy with you. He knows your name. He knows your skills. He even knows your thoughts and still loves you! Wow! He calls each of us by name – can you hear him? He loves and desires you. He has called and chosen you – are you responding to his call? In the Bible he called a young boy called Samuel. At first, Samuel didn't know it was God who had spoken his name and thought it was a priest called Eli. But when he realised that it was God who not only knew his name but wanted to speak to him, he said, "Speak Lord for I am listening." God then revealed himself to Samuel. Samuel went on to be a very significant prophet because he was able to hear God speak to him.

Today God is calling your name - do you hear him? Why not respond and tell him, "Lord I am listening!"

Respond
to
the
voice
of
God
today.

I wonder, if we were to count the number of times a day that we complain about things, would we surprise ourselves by the amount of complaints we vocalise? On the other hand, I wonder how many times per day we say we are grateful. We often forget to be grateful for things that we take for granted – like your home, your bed, your car, your food, your family, your husband/wife, your friends, your health, your strength and many more. It's only when we lose one of these things that we realise how grateful we were to have them.

I damaged three toes recently and discovered that one of them was broken. I never imagined that losing the function of three of my smallest toes was going to stop me walking for a while. I was so grateful when I started to walk again after a number of weeks. It made me realise how thankful I am to be able to go out for a simple walk. Many people are not able to walk. I had taken that ability for granted. It's so important that we highly appreciate being able to walk, talk, hear, touch, see and taste and not only appreciate these things when we lose them.

I taught an exercise at my Spiritual Health Weekend in 2022. It was to turn our complaints into grateful statements. In other words, if you say during the day, "I'm so tired", turn it into being grateful by adding, "but I am so grateful I have a bed to sleep in." If you have to walk to the shops because your parking place was so far away, turn it into a thankful thought by saying, "Although I had to walk to the shops today, I'm thankful I have two feet which are capable of walking." Saying I'm grateful each day, changes our thoughts and even changes our mood. Try it and see! It's a habit that can be life-changing.

Today – let's decide to say, "I'm grateful" many times whether it is for something small or something large. Whether it is for an item you use every day like a car, or for someone who stands with you in life like your husband/wife or friend.

I constantly go throughout my house these days telling God, "I am so grateful Lord". My husband died in 2016 and although I miss him massively, and if I could have kept him here with me I would have done so, I am so grateful to the Lord for looking after me every day in life. My grateful heart burns with thankfulness to the one who loves me so much.

Today take time to say thank you – to express your gratefulness to the one who loves and adores you.

I'm grateful
I'm thankful
I'm blessed
I'm loved
I'm accepted
I'm adored
I'm never alone
...My heart is grateful

7 Blessings for you from God!

1 LIFE - without his breath in your lungs you would die, but he doesn't just give you the ability to live, he gives you life to the full – in other words life in its best and fullest way. What a gift!

2 LOVE - not just a fragile love, but a full, free, unconditional love. God does not just give love, he is love. He gives himself to us and shows us what true love really is like.

3 JOY - not just joy for a few moments, but instead an everlasting joy that keeps bubbling up within you. He doesn't just promise you joy, but it's his joy. Jesus in John 15:7 tells us that he gives us his joy – the kind of joy that gets you through the toughest times in life. Wow!

4 PEACE - not just a sense of peace for a few moments to help us, but a peace that passes all understanding. When you are going through the toughest times on earth, you can experience his peace (the peace he says in John 14:27 that he has given to us) which when you receive it you cannot express fully to others what it is like or even understand how you can be experiencing peace at a time when life is so awful.

5 WISDOM - not just human wisdom, but wisdom that comes from Heaven itself. The Lord says he freely gives this kind of wisdom to those who ask for it. In our journey of life we all so need wisdom. We don't just need good ideas; we need God ideas. Ask him for his wisdom today.

6 HOPE - not a hope against hope, just hoping somehow you will receive what you are asking for, but instead a confident hope knowing that you will receive all you need. God has plans for each of our lives which will give us hope and a future. In Romans 15:13 it says that God is the God of all hope. Woohoo!

7 PROSPERITY - not just prosperity in worldly wealth, but he blesses you by helping you to prosper in every aspect of life. When we seek and develop intimacy with God, he guides us into prosperity – in other words his blessings are on our work, our home, our relationships, our family etc.

REMEMBER WHO YOU ARE AND WHERE GOD HAS POSTIONED YOU!

Because of his great love for us, God who is rich in mercy, made us alive with Christ even when we were dead in our transgressions – it was by grace we were saved. And God raised us up with Christ and seated us with him in the heavenly realms in Christ Jesus.

Ephesians 2:4-6

Remember who you are – someone who is loved completely and unconditionally. Someone who is called and chosen. Someone who has been made alive in Jesus, not because we deserved it, but because our God is rich in mercy and grace. When we repented and asked for forgiveness, when we gave our lives to him, and we became a Christian, he gave us something so precious and so wonderful: he accepted us and gave us the gift of eternal life. But not only that, he positioned us in a high seat, in a first class seat, in the heavenlies right next to Christ Jesus. Wow!!

We need to remember who we are and where we are positioned. We need to remember that the enemy is under our feet and that he has no dominion over us. We need to know that we have been given a seat with our name on it in the heavenlies. It's not someone else's seat; it's our seat. So, let's sit in our seat with confidence and remember we are a child of the King. Let's rejoice, remember who we are, celebrate all that God has done and enjoy living in the seat where he has placed us.

When we pray, let's remember to pray from Heaven's perspective – to pray from our seat in the heavenlies, over the situation rather than under it. Praying the same prayers and in the same way that Jesus is praying. Let's remember we have the victory in Christ Jesus and let's pray knowing that fact.

7 Reminders about you and your life

1 Your feelings are often deceptive, so do not rely on your feelings, instead rely on the truth of the word of God. Remember it's the truth that will set you free.

2 When you are going through a valley - a tough day - remember it will pass. It's as you continue to walk through your valley, that you will get to the other side.

3 Remember, you do not walk through life alone, instead you have a constant companion who absolutely loves you and is working each situation in life out for your good.

4 When shame tries to overcome you, remember that if you have asked for forgiveness, then God removes your sin as far as the east is from the west. God will never shame you - instead know that this is from the enemy, and you should tell him how free God has made you.

5 Remember you are never forgotten - who could forget someone as wonderful and precious as you? God tells us in Isaiah 49:15 that although a mother might possibly forget a precious baby at her breast, he could never forget about you!

6 The enemy of our soul will tell you that you are worthless, but the truth is you have been born to be significant - significance is your destiny!

7 When you feel ugly and unloved, look at yourself in the mirror of God's word and know that you are beautiful and deeply loved.

Look in the mirror and say:

**"You are looking at a world changer.
You are looking at a strategic person.
You were born to be significant.
You are a history maker.
You are loved and accepted.
You are more beautiful than you will ever know.
Don't ever forget how amazing you are!"**

UNBREAKABLE LOVE

Did you know that God's love for you and me is unbreakable? My husband wrote the lyrics below based on Jeremiah 33. I found these lyrics after he died and asked our daughter-in-law, Leanne Goudie, to write a melody for these words which we then recorded and released on an ep called by the same name. You can purchase a copy by going to www.ngm.org.uk/shop. God says in Jeremiah 33:20 – my paraphrase - "If you can break my covenant with the day and my covenant with the night, so that day and night no longer come at their appointed time, then my covenant of love .....with you can be broken." We cannot stop God's love for each of us - it is unbreakable!

If you could stop the day and stop the night
Remove them from their scheduled flight
Then you could stop my love for you
Erase my promise from the sky
Then you could steal the apple of my eye

Unbreakable love, unbreakable love
My love from here to eternity stretches unreservedly
Unbreakable love, unbreakable love
I am love, I am your destiny

If you could count the stars and count the sand
Reach out and hold them in your hand
Then you could count my love for you
Stop the earth from spinning round
Then you could silence heaven's loving sound

Unbreakable love, unbreakable love
My love from here to eternity stretches unreservedly
Unbreakable love, unbreakable love
I am love, I am your destiny

I'm your God, you are loved
All your failures I've restored
I'm your God, you are loved
I will never let you go

Unbreakable love, unbreakable love
My love from here to eternity stretches unreservedly
Unbreakable love, unbreakable love
I am love, I am your destiny

Are you an encourager? Are you someone who sees the potential in people and brings it out? Joseph was such a man, so much so that the people around him changed his name to Barnabus which means: son of encouragement.

When few people saw the potential in Saul of Tarsus, Barnabus took him under his wing and mentored him. Not only did Saul (whose name was then changed to Paul) become one of the greatest leaders, evangelists and teachers of the first century, but he also wrote 13 books in the Bible. At one point later when Paul did not want Mark to come on mission with him, because Mark had abandoned them in an earlier mission, Barnabus disagreed and took Mark with him on mission and encouraged and mentored him too. Again when no one saw the good in Mark, Barnabus saw it and brought it out. Mark too went on to write one of the Gospels in the Bible. Without the encouragement from Barnabus, 14 books of the New Testament may never have been written!

We all need to be a Barnabus – an encourager. Someone who sees the potential in others and draws it out of them. All of us are born to be significant – Barnabus realised this in Mark and in Paul and because of his encouragement they went on to see that God had called them to be significant.

Let's all draw out the beauty and the strength we see in others.

Do you know God?

Whether you know him or not – he knows you!

He doesn't just know about you – he deeply and intimately knows you. He knows your name. He knows how you tick. He knows your thoughts. He knows your deeds. He knows your talents. He knows your gifts. He knows your longings. He knows your desires.

He knows you!

He knows when you do things that are wrong. He knows when you do things that are kind and compassionate. He knows your generosity. He knows your fears. He knows your worries. He knows your concerns. He knows your self-less acts. He knows your selfish acts.

He knows you!

He knows your creativity. He knows your laughter. He knows your sense of humour. He knows the fun you bring. He knows what drives your passion. He knows what makes you, you!

He knows you!

He knows everything there is to know about you and guess what? He absolutely, unconditionally loves you. In fact, he lavishes his deep and wonderful love upon you - always!

Let me ask you once again – do you know God? I'm not asking whether you know about God or have read about God, or have listened to stories about God, but I'm asking do you know God intimately? Do you know his wonderful thoughts about you? Do you know his incredible plans for your life? Do you know his brilliant and wonderful love? Do you know his unconditional acceptance of you? Do you know his touch upon your life? When you do – it is life changing!

He knows you!

Don't you long to know him in a deeper and more intimate way?

Today discover the vast love of God that is deeper than an ocean and higher than the sky.

O the deep, deep love of Jesus
Vast, unmeasured, boundless, free
Rolling as a mighty ocean in its fullness over me
Underneath me, all around me, is the current
Of Thy love
Leading onward, leading homeward to
Thy glorious rest above

©. S. Trevor Francis

I pray that out of his glorious riches he may strengthen you with power through his Spirit in your inner being, so that Christ may dwell in your hearts through faith. And I pray that you, being rooted and established in love, may have power together with all the saints to grasp how wide and long and high and deep is the love of Christ, and to know this love that surpasses knowledge that you may be filled to the measure of all the fullness of God.

Ephesians 3:16-19

How great is the love the Father has lavished on us, that we should be called children of God! And that is what we are!

1 John 3:1a

Woohoo! That is who we are! Children of God. **Woohoo!** That is what he does – lavishes his love on us!

Rejoice today in the undeserved grace he pours on us.

Each and every day his beauty, joy, peace and rich life are ours to enjoy – enjoy living in his lavish love!

"You are the light of the world. A city on a hill cannot be hidden. Neither do people light a lamp and put it under a bowl. Instead, they put it on its stand, and it gives light to everyone in the house. In the same way, let your light shine before mankind, that they may see your good deeds and praise your Father in heaven."

JESUS

(Matthew 5:14-16)

You were born to be significant so, shine in the darkness and let everyone know who you are and what God has done for you!

Several years ago, my husband told me that I should write a book. I laughed and told him there was no way I could ever write a book and if he could contact my English teacher, she would back me up! However, Ray had more belief in me than I had in myself because the next time we were in a meeting with our publishers (we were in a band at the time and they produced our albums) he suddenly, without telling me, said, "Nancy has a great idea for writing a book!" I almost died! I could not believe Ray had thrown me in the deep end! However, as I began to tell them what I had been doing I noticed they were really listening. I told them about my Spiritual Health Plans that I was using with many people I was mentoring and before we left that meeting, I had a contract to do at least two books! I came out of the meeting and said to Ray, "What have you done, I cannot write a book!" However, I discovered when I sat down to write, that I absolutely loved the creativity of writing! That book went on to become my best-selling book. It was reprinted many times. In 2016, I updated it and released it again changing the title to: Nancy Goudie's Spiritual Health Encounters. I could never have imagined in my wildest dreams that I would write one book, but from that meeting with our publishers, I have written many books. The book you are now reading is my 18th book!

What I could not imagine happening, has happened because I stepped out of my comfort zone and trusted God.

I wonder what would happen to you, if you stepped out your comfort zone and trusted God?

I am significant – I can do all things through Christ who strengthens me

(Phil 4:13)

Born to be Significant

Gideon was weak and afraid, but God made him a mighty warrior!

Moses was a murderer, an angry, fear filled man, yet he became one of the most strategic leaders ever.

David was an adulterer, a murderer, yet God saw beyond his sin and loved him. David was described as a man after God's own heart.

Elijah was afraid, depressed so much that he had suicidal thoughts – yet God recommissioned him and told him the best was yet to come.

Peter denied his best friend, Jesus, three times, yet Jesus made him the foundation on which he built his church.

They were all born to be significant, yet they all failed at times – the key is they all turned to God in their failure. Have you turned to God? Have you asked for forgiveness? We all fail at times, but God knows the plans he has for our lives. Are you ready to trust him so that you too can reach your fullest potential?

YOU ARE BORN TO BE SIGNIFICANT

Do you know that God rejoices over you?

As a bridegroom rejoices over his bride, so will your God rejoice over you.

(Isaiah 62:5a)

Jesus says:

As the Father has loved me, so have I loved you. Now remain in my love.

(John 15:9)

"You are my precious gem, my beautiful diamond, my glorious and wonderful pearl.

I chose you to be mine before you ever laid eyes on me. Before you knew me, I knew you! I set you apart to be significant – so leave the cares, worries, fears and anxious moments behind and look to me. Put your hand into my hand and trust in me. I won't fail you; I won't let you down. I will take you beyond all that tears you down and bring you to a place of peace and joy. You are mine and I adore you. Never forget how much you are loved and adored. Wherever you go, I am in front of you, but I am also behind you too. I am at your right hand and your left hand; in fact, I surround you completely! Whatever you face in life, I face it with you. I am your protector, your shield, and your very great reward. Come my love and relax with me a while. Know that all that disturbs you will fade in my presence. Keep your eyes focussed on me and rest awhile with me!"

Your faithful friend-
The Lord Almighty

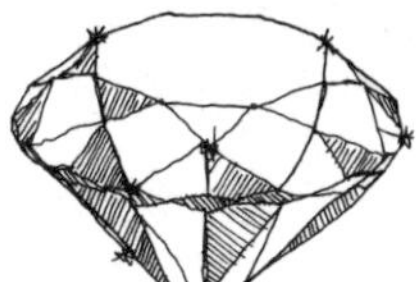

I want you to imagine you are out for a walk on a beautiful, sunny, peaceful day. You feel at peace as you feel the sun's warm rays on your body. All around you is calm and peace seems to flow through your veins. When life is treating you well it's not hard to know that God is good and kind. It's easy to see yourself as his prized possession. It's easy to know that God is good and kind and that he loves you so very much. It's not difficult to see yourself as beautiful and blessed.

But then I want you to imagine that the day becomes stormy and the winds become so strong that it seems as though the roofs of the nearby houses will be blown off. As you consider this type of day, perhaps you can feel the peace being replaced by fear and worry.

We all go through different seasons in our lives, but no matter what season you are in, remember God is unchanging. He remains good, faithful and kind to you. He continues to love you and care for you. The seasons don't change who our God is and how much he values you. He remains good, kind, loving, faithful and true to you, his beloved and precious one.

Remember, whatever season of life you are experiencing, that God loves and adores you and that he is with you always.

Choose his perfect plan for you and know the depths of his love. Hear him whisper in your ear, "You are mine and mine alone." Put away those anxious thoughts, for they do not belong here. Don't let them take up your attention and cause you pain inside. They tell you that you are locked in Winter and that the Spring will not come to you, but God tells you the truth. The winter is past and the rains are over and gone. Your anxious thoughts do not have control over your life, so dismiss them and tell them to go for you belong to another. Choose to put them aside and come and listen to the small whisper in your ear which says

- "This is the way - walk in it!"

Whether you turn to the right or to the left, your ears will hear a voice behind you saying, "This is the way; walk in it!"

Isaiah 30:21

12 things to remember when life is tough!

1. When you feel down - remember look up!

2. When you feel lonely - remember the Lord will never leave you!

3. When you feel ugly - remember you are beautiful

4. When you feel rejected - remember Jesus too was rejected

5. When you feel no one listens - remember he always hears our cries

6. When you don't understand - remember God does

7. When someone talks bad about you - remember God loves you!

8. When you feel burdened - remember he carries our burdens

9. When you are in need - remember he supplies all our needs

10. When you feel tired - remember God is your strength

11. When you feel hurt - remember he is there for you!

12. When dark clouds surround you - remember to let your light shine

When life is tough, and the road seems too difficult - remember this old hymn...

When the road is rough and steep
Fix your eyes upon Jesus
He alone has power to keep
Fix your eyes upon him.
Jesus is a gracious friend
One on whom you can depend
He is faithful to the end
Fix your eyes upon him.

Norman John Clayton

Never forget to lift your eyes and look into the eyes of the one who loves you unconditionally and has everything you could ever need.

Life looks so different when you look up!

Have you ever been in love -

truly in love where you long for the presence of the one who lights your heart and fills your life with joy? If you have ever been in love then you will recognise the urgency, the passion, the utter desperation you feel when you are apart from the one you love. Song of Songs is the story of two people in love. There is a part of the story where The Beloved searches for her love, she will not give up until she finds the love of her life. However, the one who has captured her heart was not to be found, so she asked for help in finding him. When she eventually does find him, she takes him to the place of intimacy – and she does not let him go, not for a moment (Song of Songs 3:1-4). If you read Song of Songs, you will discover that the Lover loved his Beloved so much – he calls her beautiful (Song of songs 4:1a). He woos her by telling her that she is beautiful beyond compare; to him she is absolutely flawless. He says to her, “You have stolen my heart, my sister, my bride with one glance of your eyes, with one jewel of your necklace. How delightful is your love, my sister, my bride! How much more pleasing is your love than wine…” (Song of Songs 4:9-10)

When you are in love with someone, all you need is a glance of their eyes to realise that they have stolen your heart and that there is nowhere you would rather be than in their presence.

The same is true when you come to know your Lord. His presence is something that you will search for, because once you have experienced him, nothing and no one else will ever satisfy. He is all you want and he is all you need. His love reaches to the skies. His love is deeper than the ocean. Listen and you will hear him tell you that you are beautiful, that you are glorious, that you are incredible, that you are a diamond, that you are indeed beautiful - absolutely flawless.

Remember, God does not see you or define you by your past, indeed if you have fallen in love with him and given your life to him, then your past is gone – it is forgiven. He removes it from you as far as the east is from the west. Woohoo! He does not define you by remembering your past, he has wiped it out and he remembers it no more. He looks at you as you are in the present and defines you by who you will become in the future. He sees who you are and he loves you completely and unconditionally. What a love story! What a beautiful, true story of love.

Have you fallen in love with him?
Do you long to be in his presence?
Do you have an urgency, and a passion to be near him?
Do you feel the utter desperation to go deeper with him and to hear his voice tell you that you are wonderful, incredible and his beautiful bride?

Today – fall in love with the one who first loved you – you will discover a beautiful, passionate love story that will indeed light a fire within you that will never go out – unless you allow it to do so!

Hear him call you today to deeper intimacy:

"My beloved – all beautiful you are, my darling, there is no flaw in you! Come take my hand and let's walk together in deeper intimacy. Let me show you a love that never dies. Let me whisper in your ear and bring you into a deeper intimacy. Come and experience joy that never dies and peace that flows like a river. These gifts are yours to enjoy now and in eternity. Even through heart-ache and sorrow, these gifts will never be taken away from you. Remember in this world you will have trouble but rejoice for I have overcome the world. My joy is your joy, and my peace is your peace and as I overshadow you, I bring life – life to the full. Life which is rich and free! Come my precious one – come and fall in love with me!"

When trust between two people disappears, that relationship is often very difficult to repair.

Trust is important in any relationship, but even more important in our relationship with God. Many of us have asked through the years -

Can we trust God?
Is he who he says he is?
Does he deliver on his promises?
Is he faithful, is he kind and is he trustworthy?

Throughout my life, God has shown me again and again how much he loves me – and not just me, but everyone who has ever lived. I have found him to be faithful, kind and loving; he is someone I can trust, even through the worst of times.

When my husband died after a long illness, I was in a mess! He had been my husband for 43 years; I had known him since I was 14. We started dating at 16, engaged at 18 and married at 20. He became my best friend, my partner not only in marriage, but also in ministry. We worked together for 36 years and loved doing so. When he died, I was devastated and terribly confused. So many people thought Ray would live and not die. Many Christian leaders with a healing ministry told me that they were sure he would live. Ray and I lived through so many miracles in the 20 months he was ill. We saw supernatural, amazing miracles – surely that meant that God would deliver him, but one night when I left the room for ten minutes to eat my dinner, he went to be with his Lord. He literally slept into the arms of Jesus.

That night so many questions filled my mind?
Was God not who he said he was?
What just happened?
Where were you, Lord?
I thought Ray would live and not die!
Is God not real?
Was it all a sham!

The enemy said to me, "God has turned his back on you, turn your back on him." In that moment, to be honest, I did think about it, but then I remembered the many times in my life where God had revealed himself to me and I knew I could never turn my back on him. Even though I had so many unanswered questions, I knew it was time to decide what was I going to do. Was I going to trust him even in the darkness? That night, I stood beside my bed – the bed that Ray had just died in about three hours previously and I spoke out loud to my God. I told him, "Lord I have 101 different questions and I don't have the answer to any of them. I don't understand what has just happened, but I want to tell you, that I know I am not called to understand everything that happens in life, but I am called to trust you and trust you is what I am going to do."

That decision to trust God when darkness, confusion and pain was all around was the best thing I have ever done, apart from trusting God when I became a Christian at 6 years of age. God heard my words and he helped me to walk through the valley of the shadow of death. He gave me the gift of the kind of peace that passes all understanding and also what I called a bubble of joy. Both those gifts have never left me. His amazing presence remains with me to this day – he has indeed been faithful and true. He never leaves me; he never forsakes me. It hasn't always been easy, but I have felt his presence with me and that has enabled me to overcome the darkness. The wonderful thing is that he does this for everyone who will dare to trust him! Will you trust him in the darkness and allow his light and his beauty to shine through you?

Jesus says:
"In this world you will have trouble but take heart I have overcome the world."

John 16:33

Trust him and you will discover his unfailing love for you, his beautiful and significant child.

trust

Several years ago, I was asked by Christian Aid to go to Uganda with a few Christian leaders to present a video of the work they were doing in that nation. During filming, I interviewed a woman who had absolutely nothing! She lived in a very small mud hut with no furniture. She had to sit on the dirty, mud floor. She looked as though she was in her late 70's but I discovered that she was only 50! The day we arrived she had no money to buy food for herself and her family. She began to explain to me about her life and the more I heard, the more I expected her to be forlorn and broken, but it wasn't long before her face began to glow as she spoke about Jesus. She told me she was so grateful for all God had given her. I thought to myself, how can she be so grateful when she has nothing.

It made me realise that we who live in the UK have so much, yet many of us live our lives without being grateful and without thankfulness in our hearts. I have a bed, a king-sized bed to sleep in. I have a home with several bedrooms and a living room. All she had was a mud hut – one where we wouldn't even keep a dog! Even though her life was stricken with problems, her face glowed with the presence of Jesus. That woman had no cash or possessions, but she had treasure within, and she couldn't help but express her genuine gratefulness. It made me realise that, even though she was surrounded by poverty, she was rich and it was me/us who live in the West who are the poorer. She had nothing yet she had everything – she was significant and made a huge impact on me and the whole team in Uganda.

What about you?
Are you grateful for all you have?

The more I experience of life, the more grateful I have become. Every day I take time to express my gratitude not only for all I have but for the one who never leaves me or forsakes me. The one whose presence has impacted my life and I choose not to live without. Let's develop a thankful heart. Let's express our gratefulness every day. In doing so we will make an impact not only on those around us but on ourselves too.

NB.....did you know that being grateful can boost neurotransmitter serotonin and activate the brain to produce dopamine (the brain's pleasure chemical). The more we develop gratitude and positive thoughts, the healthier and happier we will become.

So, then, just as you received Christ Jesus as Lord, continue to live in him, rooted and built up in him, strengthened in the faith as you were taught, and overflowing with thankfulness.

Colossians 2: 6-7

Be joyful always; pray continually, give thanks in all circumstances, for this is God's will for you in Christ Jesus.

1 Thessalonians 16-18

If you have ever heard me speak you will, I'm sure, have heard me say that there are three steps mentioned in the Bible that develop faith: Hearing, Obeying and Trusting. You may also have heard me say that my late husband and I, and the whole of the ngm ministry, have lived by faith for our finances for the last 43 years. That has meant that we have had to trust God for everything we need. This has been such a privilege as we have seen God move miraculously again and again. It has not always been easy, and in fact a lot of the times it has been tough, but we have learned so much and God has never failed us yet.

At one point in my life, just after my husband died, a very kind friend gave me a gift of a two-night break in a hotel in the north. When two of my friends realised that I would be at the hotel on my own they booked in for a night to join me. What a joy those two days were – I loved my time with them. We had such fun. On the first night we had a meal at one of the restaurants at the hotel and one of my friends paid for it. On the second night, I was by myself and I wondered what to do for my meal. As we had been at one of the restaurants for the previous night and I had seen how it seemed a little difficult for a woman on her own to be there, I chose the other restaurant which seemed a little more formal, but so much quieter. When I arrived for my meal, I was asked to first of all go into the bar and I would receive a menu. I ordered a glass of wine but when I looked at the menu, I had a big shock. I hadn't checked online to see what the menu was as I had decided just to have a main meal with no starters or desert so that I would not have too much to pay, however the menu told me that they only had Taster Menus. They gave you a choice of a three-course taster menu, a six-course taster menu, or a nine-course taster menu. The three-course taster menu was about £75 and it went up from there! I panicked. I didn't know what to do. Should I just leave before they come to take my order?

Then I thought they had already seen me and, as I am staying in the hotel, they would ring the room. I thought I could always ask if I could go to the other restaurant, but without a reserved table I might not get in. In the middle of my troubled thoughts God spoke and said, "Nancy just relax and enjoy it! Trust me!" So, I decided to do so. I ordered the three-course Taster meal and decided to trust God.

When it came time for me to leave the hotel, I went to ask for my bill. Obviously, my accommodation had been paid by my kind friend, so I should only have the previous night's meal to pay. When I got the bill the only thing on it was my glass of wine. I told her that I had been in the restaurant for a meal the previous evening and the cost of that meal should be on the bill. She went away and checked it for me and came back saying there was nothing on the system for my meal. I asked her if someone else could have paid it for me. I was thinking perhaps one of my two friends the previous evening had called and covered the cost. She said it was quite possible, but there was nothing else to pay other than the wine. I got her to check twice and then paid for the glass of wine and left. I obviously wanted to thank my friends for the meal and so I called them both and asked if they had paid it; neither of them had. I don't know what happened about my meal, but as I had heard, obeyed and trusted God – he dealt with it!

These kinds of things have happened to me again and again. One time many years ago, we went to have a holiday in Lincolnshire. We pre-paid the accommodation and all we had to pay at the end of our week's break was the electricity. We paid that and left having had a wonderful time in a lodge with our friends. When my credit bill came in, the cost of the accommodation was not on it. I called them and enquired about it, but they told me that it might be too early to get it. Month after month I enquired about it when the bill still did not appear. Eventually the company checked it and told me that there was no note of us ever having stayed at the resort. I told them we had paid the electricity and could they check again. They then told me "Mrs Goudie, please don't call us again!" We never did get the bill. Believe it or not, that happened to us again the following year!

Just this year when I stayed at a hotel, I noticed an item on my bill which was incorrect. I pointed it out to the receptionist who went away to check it and came back saying it was impossible for her to check if it was correct and to just pay what was on the bill! It should have been over £100 more expensive! I realise other people can sometimes have this happen to them, but these 'co-incidences' seem to happen to me and to others I know who live by faith for their finances, again and again. God is faithful to all his promises. When he says to trust him – never be afraid to do so.

God's word to you, his beautiful one, his beloved!

"Listen to me....you whom I have upheld since you were conceived, and have carried since your birth. Even to your old age and grey hairs I am he, I am he who will sustain you. I have made you and I will carry you; I will sustain you and I will rescue you."

Isaiah 46:3-4

The God who made the universe, lovingly and wonderfully made you – he cares for you and watches over you – never forget that from birth to your old age, he pours his love, his adoration, and his strength on you. His watchful eye is always on you! How wonderful he is!

When you truly know him, you never want to live a moment without him and his wonderful presence!

Since ancient times no one has heard, no ear has perceived, no eye has seen any God besides you, who acts on behalf of those who gladly do right and who remember your ways.

Isaiah 64:4-5

No eye has seen, no ear has heard, no mind has conceived what God has prepared for those who love him

I Corinthians 2:9

"For I know the plans I have for you," declares the Lord, "plans to prosper you and not to harm you, plans to give you hope and a future."

Jeremiah 29:11

His plans for our lives are beyond our wildest dreams WOOHOO Trust him always!

You are God's special and wonderful creation; he placed you in his delight.

Did you know that when God created Adam and Eve he placed them in a wonderful, beautiful, colourful garden filled with abundant provision called Eden? I discovered that another word for Eden is delight or pleasure. I then saw in the dictionary it said that Eden meant 'a place of delight/a state of perfect happiness or bliss'. Wow! What a wonderful truth to discover! God placed his beautiful creation in an amazing garden – in his delight – in his pleasure. They were surrounded by delight, they were covered by delight and no matter where they looked, they saw and breathed delight. They lived in a place of perfect bliss. Wow! God loved mankind so much that he positioned them to live in his joy, pleasure and delight. This experience was not just for Adam and Eve, as we too have been placed in his wonderful all-encompassing delight.

Zephaniah 3:17 tells us that God takes great delight in each of us. He rejoices over us with singing and finds much pleasure in you and in me! Wow! We are not worthless creatures. Indeed, before we were born, God poured his delight into us. Even before we took our first breath, he was drenching us with his love and pleasure. You and I were created to live, breathe and be covered daily with his delight. The Bible tells us that no matter who we are, each of us is a person of great worth and immense value. There is an invitation to all of us to explore and come to know the depths of his amazing love and delight.

The truth is that none of us earned his delight, neither did we deserve his grace or favour, but every day we walk, run and live in his glorious delight. The truth is we cannot go anywhere without his love covering us. The very air that we breathe has been given to us from above. If he ever removed his breath from us, we would all die.

In the Bible (Joshua 18:3) Joshua challenges Israel to take a hold of what God has already given them. He says, "How long will you wait before you begin to take possession of the land God has given you?" The same could be asked of each of us. "How long are you going to take before you begin to experience real life?" He tells us each day that he loves us, yet how long are we going to wait until we experience the depth of his love and pleasure? He tells us in the Bible that he delights in us, yet how many of us live experiencing that enormous delight? He tells us that we are loved and valued – that we were chosen even before the foundation of the world was put in place, yet how many of us think of ourselves as worthless? Jesus came to this earth to give us freedom, yet how many of us live in freedom from fear, worry and concern? How long will we live with our negative thoughts and words? Why do we allow our fears to stop us from living in the land of freedom and joy? How long will we wait before experiencing what God has freely given us – joy, peace, life and freedom? Today, let's choose to live and enjoy his delight and pleasure and let's choose this day to welcome his love into our hearts.

Today I choose you Lord and receive all you have for me!

"Come to me, all you who are weary and burdened, and I will give you rest."
JESUS

Matthew 11:28

If you confess with your mouth "Jesus is Lord" and believe in your heart that God raised him from the dead, you will be saved.
For it is with your heart that you believe and are justified, and it is with your mouth that you confess and are saved.

Romans 10:9-10

May the God of hope fill you with all joy and peace as you trust in him, so that you may overflow with hope by the power of the Holy Spirit.

Romans 15:13

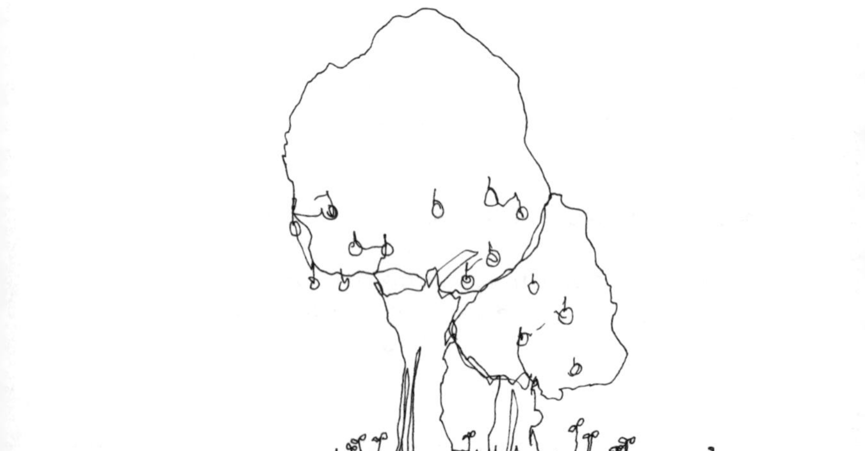

You are born to be significant

For you created my inmost being - you knit me together in my mother's womb. I praise you because I am fearfully and wonderfully made; your works are wonderful; I know that full well.

My frame was not hidden from you when I was made in the secret place. When I was woven together in the depths of the earth, your eyes saw my unformed body.

All the days ordained for me were written in your book before one of them came to be.

How precious to me are your thoughts O God! How vast the sum of them! Were I to count them, they would outnumber the grains of the sand.

Psalm 139:13-18a

**Remember how precious you are;
you were born to be significant.**

You are beautiful and significant

There is nothing that you and
he cannot do together!

So remember every day of
your life, no matter how you
are feeling or what situation
you find yourself in ....

........you are beautiful and you were born to be significant!

About the Author

Nancy Goudie is a well-known speaker and author. She and her late husband formed the band 'Heartbeat' in the 80's and went on to found NGM and The Inspire Arts Trust based at Caedmon (their multi-million-pound arts and music complex in Thornbury, Bristol, England). Nancy has written 18 books and recorded 6 meditation CD's and 2 Bible/Prayer CD's. She has also founded Nancy Goudie's Spiritual Health Weekends in the UK and Spain held in 4 and 5 star luxury hotels. She holds Spiritual Health Days in various parts of the UK and beyond. She is regularly on TV and Radio and has developed her own podcast plus a new online programme on faith for men and women. Nancy speaks at conferences, events and churches in various parts of the world.

For more information on Nancy's ministry or to book her to come to your area, please visit:

www.nancygoudie.com
or www.ngm.org.uk

Nancy Goudie's
Spiritual Health Weekends | UK

One life changing weekend in a stunning 4-star hotel!

This is a weekend like no other. It's a place for women of all ages to be pampered physically yet toned up spiritually at the same time. You will feel special from the moment you arrive to the moment you leave! Come and see for yourself what this wonderful, spectacular and unique weekend is all about. This is a God appointment for you!

Nancy Goudie has been running these luxury, unique and sensational weekend conferences for the last 25 years at 4-star luxury hotels in the UK. Why not join Nancy for: Nancy's inspiring and life-changing teaching, powerful and intimate worship from the ngm worship band, inspiring input from special guests, pampering experiences, 5 star entertainment, special individual words from God, creative optional sessions, a God perfumed prayer room and so much more!

Worried you can't afford the cost? Talk to us about spreading your payments. You can also apply for a subsidised place through our bursary scheme.

Don't miss out! This is a precious God appointment for you!

What people say:

"There is nothing else like this, it's wonderful." **J.H**

"I felt God tell me that it was a privilege to attend these weekends. When I came to the first one many years ago, the love and care I felt then is still as strong 15 years later!" **SS**

For more information and booking details

visit www.nancygoudie.com or call 01454 414880

Nancy Goudie's
Spiritual Health Weekends | **SPAIN**

This is a Spiritual Health Weekend like no other!

How about spending a long weekend in the south of Spain in a 5 star luxury hotel, where you learn to cook Paella (optional), exercise on the beach (optional), eat out at a nice restaurant and lie in the sun, but at the same time have worship and teaching and discover God in a deeper and more intimate way? The resort has four swimming pools, gorgeous rooms and apartments, a beautiful restaurant and a lovely sandy beach too. Every time we have held this weekend, the ladies have all said they would come back. They loved the resort, loved the company and loved the teaching. Each year the weather has been stunning and God has moved in healing as well as transforming hearts and lives. You will love this weekend in the sun, so come and join us.

What people say:

"This is the second time I have been to Nancy Goudie's Spiritual Health Weekend in Spain and I absolutely loved it. I've been to Windsor and I've been to Preston but this is a new level altogether."
S.L Delegate

Other Paperback Books and Products

by Nancy Goudie. Available at www.nancygoudie.com

Who Would Ever Have Thought

This is the incredible story of two ordinary people from Ayr in Scotland. They lived in an idyllic and beautiful bungalow, had terrific jobs as well as a brand new sporty car, had a myriad of wonderful friendships and brilliant families too, but they left it all behind to follow God on what turned out to be an amazing faith filled journey. It's the story of Heartbeat, ngm, Caedmon – their £3 million pound arts facility, Nancy's Spiritual Health Weekends, Ray's musicals luv esther, The Prodigals and much, much more. Nancy takes you through the highs as well as the lows, yet once you've finished reading, you'll be left feeling encouraged and built up. There are many places where you will laugh and a few where you may shed a tear! This is not just a story; this is a journey that will change your life. **Also available on Amazon Kindle and audiobook (via Audible)**

Spiritual Health Encounters

This unique and creative book helps you to spend time in the secret place and will transform and deepen your intimacy with God. Each practical exercise takes you on an exciting, creative journey of mediation, hearing from heaven, writing a psalm and real encounters with God. It's great for individuals, small groups and for counsellors/disciplers to give to those who need to see a breakthrough. This is a dynamic book that can really change lives! **Also available on Amazon Kindle.**

Our Greatest Adventure

This book tells a story of courage in the midst of pain, peace in the midst of sorrow and trust in the midst of confusion. It's a story of love and devotion in the midst of one of the biggest challenges Ray and Nancy Goudie have ever known. It's the story of God's faithfulness when Ray was diagnosed as having pancreatic cancer and of God's continued faithfulness and immense presence when Ray walked through the valley of the shadow of death and eventually fell asleep into the arms of Jesus. This is an honest, deep and raw story that will touch your emotions, making you laugh as well as cry. There are many funny and humorous moments amidst the pain and the heartache. It's a story that will fuel your faith in God and ignite your passion for his presence. This is a story that many have said had to be told. **Also available on Amazon Kindle.**

Treasures of Darkness

This is a very naked and honest autobiographical account of a time when the world around Nancy started to collapse. Her husband, Ray, fell into a dark pit where he experienced ill health and burnout. At the same time God was taking their ministry, ngm, through a shift, which caused much pain and insecurity and led to many people eventually leaving. Pressures swept in like a storm leaving devastation, confusion and unanswered prayers. Nancy discovered that through this time there were *'treasures of darkness and riches hidden in a secret place'* (Isaiah 45:3).

Special offer when you buy all three

The Beloved (hardback book)

This is a collection of real stories, poems, wise words, meditations and huge encouragement to know that you are God's beloved child. Any time you are feeling down, unloved, criticised or critical of yourself and life hits you hard, then pick up this book and flick through its pages. Each page is designed to bring you words of encouragement, hope and love.

Confident? (hardback book)

This book is for anyone who sometimes swings from being confident to feeling a failure. It's a book full of encouragement, wise words, poems, songs and stories to lift your spirit and get you back on your feet again, ready to face life once more. Through its pages you will feel accepted, really loved and realise afresh how amazing you are!

You are Special (hardback book)

In our culture of stress with so much pressure to look good and be famous, we often need to be reminded just how unique, precious, remarkable and extraordinary we are! No matter what colour our skin is, what size we are, what intelligence we display, what background we come from, the truth is each of us is an exceptional human being. In every page of this book you will discover the truth about yourself and realise afresh that you are deeply loved, special and accepted.

Special offer when you buy together

Oasis of Hope (hardback book)

There are times in our lives when we all need an oasis, a place where we can go and receive a thirst quenching drink for our souls. This book is such a place! A place where hope is renewed and faith can begin to grow. A place that will help refresh the reader physically, mentally, emotionally and spiritually. A place that gives us more of what we need to enable us to keep on going in our journey through life. It is designed to plant seeds of hope into the barren places of our hearts and encourage those seeds to grow and develop so that our faith will soar.

Oasis of Delight (hardback book)

There are times in our lives when we need an oasis, a place where we can go to receive a thirst quenching drink for our souls. This book is an exploration of what it means to live in the oasis of delight, tasting its fruit, relaxing and relishing in the lush surroundings; free to explore and enjoy the depths of his fulness of joy and his pleasures forevermore. It inspires us to enjoy the delightful fruit of intimacy with God, whilst all the time pointing us towards the day when we will be in the ultimate garden of delight for eternity.

The Best Is Yet To Come Journal

This fantastic journal has a page of inspiration from Nancy and plenty of pages for your notes, prayers, drawings etc. Printed with a luxury finish this is the ideal journal for you – grab your copy now.

All books are available direct from ngm at:

www.ngm.org.uk/shop, www.nancygoudie.com
or through **www.amazon.co.uk**

Meditation CDs

Peace Like a River

If you have ever experienced stress, carried worries, fought fears or are just looking for an oasis in your busy life, then this CD is for you. This recording will take you to a place of tranquillity, where peace, love and grace are yours in abundance. Use this CD daily and you will find peace like a river flowing through your soul. **Also available to download from iTunes and other online platforms.**

Smile

If you are feeling the daily stresses of life, the busyness of work, the pressures of family or just need some soothing for your soul, then this is recording for you. **Also available to download from iTunes and other online platforms.**

Meditations for the Beloved

We all need to know we are loved and valued. This incredible music and mediation CD will take you to the secret place where you will know you are The Beloved; you will be overwhelmed with love, feel accepted and experience a peace that passes all understanding. **Also available to download from iTunes and other online platforms.**

Speak...Declare the Truth: Vol 1

Are you feeling overwhelmed? Are circumstances or people getting you down? Are you in need of encouragement? Do you need to know you are loved? Do you need to see a miracle of health or provision? Does everything seem impossible for you? Then I have news for you! The Bible says in 2 Peter 1:3 that God has already given you everything you need for life and godliness. Not just some things, but everything you need. We need to start reading, believing and confessing the truth. This CD helps you to do just that!

What we speak has power and therefore when we confess the truth contained in the word of God, power is released and the word brings life. Speak life and truth into your circumstances and let's see God do a miracle! **Also available to download from iTunes and other online platforms.**

Speak...Declare the Truth: Vol 2

Do you know you are loved? Do you realise you are valued? Do you understand you are special? So many of us struggle with confidence, our self-image and our mental ability to believe we are worthy. We don't value ourselves and therefore we cannot see how anyone else will value us. Do you know God delights in you and celebrates you? Do you realise that he sings songs of joy and delight over you? Do you struggle with the ability to see a joyful future full of hope? God not only believes in you but he has wonderful plans and purposes for your life. Who are you listening to? Who are you believing? We need to listen to the truth of the word of God rather than listening to the lies of the enemy.

There is power in the spoken word, so read, believe and confess the truth and see your circumstances and your life change for the better. **Also available to download from iTunes and other online platforms.**

All meditation cds are available direct from ngm at:

www.ngm.org.uk/shop, www.nancygoudie.com
or through **www.amazon.co.uk**

Other Products

Bible Reading Planners

A superb way of systematically reading through the Bible in one or two years.

Wholehearted - by Leanne Goudie

Wholehearted is a 30-day interactive devotional written by Leanne Goudie and packed full of encouragements, scriptures and space to journal. So many women go through life struggling to embrace their God given identity and worth, so Wholehearted was written to encourage and equip women in their everyday lives. **Also available on Amazon Kindle.**

Throughout the book there is space to journal and write, allowing you to process anything that arises from reading the encouragement given each day. This is your devotional and your space to process, so take it at your own pace and enjoy the journey of living your life. Grab your copy now!

Rooted - by Leanne Goudie

Rooted was created to help you delve deeper into what it is to truly trust God and encourage you to look at how you can live a life of complete faith in Him. Throughout there is space for you to journal and process anything that arises from reading the encouragement given each day. This is your devotional and your space, so take it at your own pace and embrace the journey of becoming more and more 'Rooted' in your faith!

One Woman's Guide to Life - Zoe Wickham

At the time of writing this book I am 43 years old. I haven't lived all my years but I feel I have lived enough, and learned some life lessons the hard way, so I want to share them with others. My heart is that you will find freedom in these pages, you will be free to express who you were born to be, you will discover it's not too late to change things no matter what age you are, you will learn to take care of yourself and learn also that it's okay not have all the answers. I have read a lot of self-help books (there's nothing wrong with them) in the journey of trying to improve myself, but this isn't one of those. This is an honest account from a wife, a mum, a woman who has lived her first 40 plus years and wants to share with you some of the highs and lows to help you to find balance, happiness and joy in life and that you might learn to live life more fully!

NGM Worship - Unbreakable Love

Unbreakable Love featuring the beautiful vocals of Leanne and Esther. This is a great ep with some fantastic new songs, plus a re-release of the track Heal Our Nation from Heartbeat. Do make sure you grab your copy for yourself and for your family/friends!

You can purchase all of these products direct from ngm at:

www.ngm.org.uk/shop, www.nancygoudie.com
or through **www.amazon.co.uk**

NANCY GOUDIE CONTACT DETAILS:

Should you wish to contact Nancy,
then you can write to her at:

nancy@nancygoudie.com

ngm,
Caedmon Complex,
Bristol Road,
Thornbury, BS35 3JA

Facebook: Nancy Goudie
Twitter: @nancygoudie
Instagram: @nancygoudie
YouTube: Nancy Goudie – NGM Trust

If you wish to find out more about anything in the book
or request prayer you can call: 01454 414880

For more information on Nancy and all she is doing
visit www.nancygoudie.com